MUSIC LESSONS FOR THE MAN IN THE PEW

Contents

Chapter 1	Why Sing	3
Chapter 2	Singing Our Best	
	Why Sing Well	16
	The Voice — a Musical Instrument	17
	Making the Most of the Natural Voice	22
	Sustained Speech	23
	A Modern Singing Aid	26
Chapter 3	Sight-reading Melodies	
	Why Johnny Can't Read Music	27
	Do - A Deer	31
	How to Find Do in a Song	36
	Intervals	42
	Sharps and Flats	43
Chapter 4	Rhythm	
	Beats and Time Measurement	48
	Time Signatures	56
	The Tie and the Dotted Notes	57
	Rests	61
Chapter 5	The Songs We Sing	
	Our Background	63
	Hymns	64
	Source of Our Present Hymns	66
	Psalms	73
Chapter 6	Why We Don't Sing	75

Chapter 1
WHY SING

You step into a Catholic Church these days, and before you can even get the kink out of your genuflecting knee, they hand you a hymnal, and from then on it's "come on now, everybody sing!" The Church is no longer a place to get peace and quiet and prayer. It's no wonder these sacred sing-alongs are sometimes called "Hymnenannies."

This is probably what a lot of Catholics have been thinking now that the Liturgy is changed and continues to change until it becomes the full expression of today's people of God singing his praise. So when you say you can't pray at Mass these days, you are right, if by prayer you mean the personal, private prayer between you and God alone. Surely you've heard by this time that the Mass is a community worship, an assembly called together by God to offer his praise in Christ.

The Second Vatican Council has declared that "in the Liturgy the whole public worship is performed by the mystical body of Jesus Christ, that is, by the head and his members." "Liturgical services are not private functions, but a celebration of the Church, which is the 'Sacrament of Unity,' namely, the holy people united and ordered under their bishops." "Christ is present, when the Church prays and sings, for he promised: 'where two or three are gathered together in my name, there

NOBODY'S LOOKING

am I in the midst of them.'" And lastly, ".... all who are made
sons of God by faith and baptism should come together to
praise God in the midst of his Church, to take part in the
sacrifice, and to eat the Lord's supper." Now certainly "two
or three gathered together in my name" does not mean two
or three people kneeling side by side each offering his private
prayers. And the sons of God coming together to praise God
in the midst of his Church and eating the Lord's supper certainly implies that we do this together as a family in God's
household.

The Vatican Council furthermore declares, "Liturgical
worship is given a more noble form when the Divine Offices
are celebrated solemnly in song, with the assistance of sacred
ministers and the active participation of the people." It is this
very "active participation in song" with which this book is
concerned.

That you should be called to the role of a singer may still
be hard to accept. You didn't apply for the job, but nevertheless, you're hired. You've been drafted. The "don't call us,

we'll call you" bit now has an ecclesiastical application. You're called!

You may have never made the school glee club or the parish choir, and maybe in kindergarten you were a bluebird rather than a canary. Nevertheless, you're a singer now! Pope Paul and the Vatican Council imply that you are. So did Pope John, Pope Pius, and a lot of other popes before them all the way back to Peter. They were not acting the part of amateur talent scouts, they were speaking in the name of Jesus Christ himself.

"Let the full harmonious singing of our people," says Pope Pius XII, rise to heaven like the bursting of a thunderous sea and let them testify by the melody of their song to the unity of their hearts and minds, as becomes brothers and the children of the same Father."

Calling you a singer then does not infer that you are a "diva," a "prima donna," or an operatic tenor; you're too slim and much too modest. The special role in which you are

YOU TOLD ME YOURSELF THAT YOU WERE A "CANARY" IN KINDERGARTEN

cast types you not as a concert soloist, but simply as a normal human being carrying on the natural function of praising and thanking the God who made you. Again, Pope Pius XII speaks: "A congregation that is devoutly present at the Sacrifice, in which our Saviour together with his children redeemed with his Sacred Blood sings the nuptial hymn of his immense love, cannot keep silent for 'song befits the lover' and, as the ancient saying has it, 'he who sings well prays twice.' Thus the Church militant, faithful as well as clergy, joins in the hymns of the Church triumphant and with the choirs of angels, and, all together, sing a wondrous and eternal hymn of praise to the most Holy Trinity in keeping with the words of the Preface: 'With whom our voices too thou wouldst bid to be admitted.'"

THE
POPE
SAYS
SING

"Couldn't I do all this by just talking rather than singing," you might ask (and we hope you do ask, so we might answer you as follows:) Yes, you could—just as every Broadway musical could be a stage play, every lover could speak "Let me call you sweetheart" instead of singing it; and so could every child and adult simply recite "Happy birthday to you" rather than gift-wrapping these words in the gay ribbon and glorious colors of song.

The word "Alleluia," that wonderful exclamation of holy joy, almost loses its meaning when it is spoken rather than sung. Try it once as an experiment. Speak your words several times then sing them several times, even making your own happy melody if you wish. Try reciting "Happy birthday to you," and then sing it. It just is not the same. Song has that happy faculty of clothing words in the beautiful apparel of melody, enhancing them in harmony, intensifying them, and making them more attractive and appealing — and in the case of sung prayer — probably more effective.

Pius XII has said, "since the principal office (of music) is to clothe with simple melody the liturgical text proposed for the understanding of the faithful, its proper aim is to add greater efficacy to the text, in order that through it the faithful may be more easily moved to devotion and better disposed for the reception of the fruits of grace belonging to the celebration of the most holy mysteries."

"Miraculously preserved unharmed in the Red Sea by God's power, the people of God sang a song of victory to the Lord, and Miriam, the sister of Moses, their leader, endowed with prophetic inspiration, sang with the people while playing a tambourine."

"The dignity and lofty purpose of sacred music consist in the fact that its lovely melodies and splendor beautify and embellish the voices of the priest who offers Mass and the Christian people who praise the sovereign God. Its special power and excellence should lift up to God the minds of the faithful who are present. It should make the liturgical prayers of the Christian community more alive and fervent so that everyone can praise and beseech the Triune God more powerfully, more intently and more effectively."

Now all these glorious flights of rhetoric about song, fruitful and inspiring as they are, need *you* to bring them to their full realization. *You* are the one who must give practical value to all these eloquent truths regarding the sung liturgy that were uttered by pontiffs and saints and Christ himself.

Were you to respond to these invitations of the Church to sing by answering, "I can't sing," "I have no voice," you would then — unless you are an exception to normal humanity in this respect — be inferring that the church is wrong in rashly presuming that the average person in the pew can sing.

Again we wish to remind you that the "singing" we refer to is not "concert singing," especially not "solo" singing. It is the singing of you and your brethren joined together in Christ and praying in song; members of the Body of Christ, singing now as Christ and his twelve apostles did immediately after they had eaten the "Last Supper" and "after having sung a hymn they went out to the Mount of Olives."

In the Christian community even a "bad voice" or an "off-key" voice has its place. It is not "listening music" except for God's ear and his ear obviously discerns sincerity and well-meaning efforts above an appealing sound.

Besides, the particular ingredient that a poor voice adds to the combined sounds of a mighty chorus may be the precise little touch that will perfect the recipe, just as a pungent spice, which by itself would bite or sting the tongue, might be the crowning flavor when directly added to an Epicurean dish.

We've all heard priests at the altar who couldn't sing. But did we really mind? A priest offers our gifts to God in elevated tones, and who does it really bother if he's flat? A choir is different. These singers, by virtue of their function, aspire to artistic perfection. But a priest and congregation, no! Uninhibited sincerity is the one prerequisite.

So sing! Sing from the heart! It is not the voice that really sings; it is the heart! Many a star of Broadway shows can put over a song in spite of his lack of a "voice." You can put over your song with God too! You'll never find a more appreciative audience.

SINGING OUR BEST

WHY SING WELL?

Now, in spite of all that has been said up to this point, and certainly without any intention to contradict it, we the people in the pew, must do all in our power to present our sung prayer before the throne of our Father in heaven in a most worthy and fitting manner. In short, we must sing our best. When we recite the Lord's Prayer and the Hail Mary it is obvious that to do so in a murmuring inarticulate fashion is distracting and undevotional. The same holds true for singing these prayers.

MMFFLF
NOPHLAM
MNIOLF
MNUFFIX

The degree of our devotion at Mass may depend upon the manner in which we sing our prayers. Still remembering that sincerity and freedom from inhibitions are the keynote, we must not only sing devoutly and reverently but with the best possible artistry. To achieve this end, this booklet is written. In the following pages we shall endeavor to briefly give a few simple and untechnical music lessons both in the reading of notes and in the use of the voice in singing.

THE VOICE — A MUSICAL INSTRUMENT

Ask any group of children, or adults for that matter, what is their favorite musical instrument. The answers will usually indicate the piano, violin, organ, or a few other standard instruments, (the guitar especially in the present decade of our culture). The unsuspecting children (and anyone who has not read the caption of this paragraph) would completely forget about the human voice as an instrument. Again no one stated this truth better than the Vicar of Christ. "No instrument," says Pope Pius XI, "however perfect, however excellent, can

surpass the human voice in expressing human thought, especially when it is used by the mind to offer up prayer and praise to Almighty God."

There we have it! The human voice is the greatest musical instrument ever invented! Science supports this statement of Pope Pius XI. Scientists, with their up-to-date gadgets and laboratories can measure sound waves with graphs and wavy lines; but eventually they arrive at the same conclusion as Holy Father: "No instrument is as great as the human voice."

Let's face it, you're a walking piano, a breathing violin, a living guitar!

However, our human instrument, the voice, is not one that can be toted around in a portable case like a violin or guitar. Much more than the ankle bone is connected to the knee bone is the voice connected to us. It is inseparable from us; it is intimately a part of us. So much so that our every mood, our every emotion is reflected in it. Did you ever notice: when someone is angry, you can tell it in his voice; when someone is sad, you can tell it in his voice; and when someone is frightened he can even lose his voice. Doesn't it follow then that when someone is happy it is also reflected in his voice? And don't you think that sincerity, love, and perhaps even humility are somehow the undisguised overtones in one's speech and in one's song? Talk about your temperamental opera stars, "great" singers whose tantrums are sometimes recorded on the front pages of our newspapers! My suspicions are that the "temperament" is merely a phony cover-up for a lack of true talent and greatness; that pride and affectation reverberate through their voices, and that the "greatness" of these artists must be accepted only on the compelling basis of fame, and the extravagant claims of press agents. These truths are caught somehow in the frank reply of a little boy who, when asked how he liked the singing of a certain famous would-be star exclaimed, "It sure is beautiful; but I don't like it." He knew that his voice, according to popular acclaim and reputation was supposed to be good; but in his childlike candor, he could not agree with adult public opinion.

On the other hand, all the truly glorious voices this writer has heard in his lifetime were invariably possessed by magnanimous persons whose humility and genuineness matched the magnitude of their great God-given talent. Somehow you feel that they *are* magnanimous people, not *in spite* of their talent or *because of it;* rather they are a great talent because of their magnanimity.

Of course, the ratio of virtue and talent is much too moot a problem to be settled here, especially since the inspiration — and we presume, the gift — of the Holy Spirit blows where it will; and more often the talents are bestowed upon the scoundrel, rather than upon the saint. Nor do we mean to imply that St. Peter will judge your eligibility to pass through heaven's gates by simply asking you to open your mouth wide and sing "ah."

We merely wish to give credence to Pius XI's statement and to realize the import of its truth in our own lives; that our own human voice, be it the rare concert variety, or the simply mediocre voice of the average man in the pew, is still an unsurpassed musical instrument. Further more, a natural voice, untrained (or unruined) by professional singing lessons, is not only adequate for the purpose, but it is pre-eminently suited for expressing the sentiments of one's mind and heart in an unsophisticated manner.

Also we wish to point out that the attitude and mood of the singer has a profound influence on the sound of his voice. If a man in a church pew is afraid of being heard by the person beside him, he has already pre-doomed his best intentions to sing well. He will sound scared. However, if he learns to conquer his inhibitions, he will produce a better tone. Or we can just as well say, if he learns to produce a good singing tone, he already has learned to overcome his self-consciousness. The mental and vocal mastery go hand in hand.

This psychological approach to voice production has too often been neglected even by the best professional voice teachers. They forget that after all one might really sing best in the bath tub.

MAKING THE MOST OF THE NATURAL VOICE

Naturalness is better in everything — the golfer's swing, the batter's stance, the swimmer's stroke — all artists, all athletes strive after naturalness. The trouble is, athletes must work extremely hard to achieve this natural way of doing things. They even have to call in outside coaches to help them attain this naturalness. So it is with the voice. Sometimes it is so difficult to rid ourselves of mental blocks, of physical habits that might interfere with our best natural tones.

Singing lessons can hardly be given in a correspondence course, much less in these brief chapters devoted to the *natural* singing voice. We would simply like to emphasize a few principles that may be somewhat self-evident.

The chief difference between talking and speaking is evident from the following truths:

a) Singing is simply sustained speech.

b) This speech is sustained on various but precise pitches. Our reader may demonstrate these principles by first reciting and then singing a familiar hymn such as "Holy God, We Praise Thy Name."

SUSTAINED SPEECH

It is imperative to know that it is the vowel in a syllable or word that is sustained or prolonged, and not the consonant. For example, sing the word "fair," sustaining the vowel for a few seconds, making sure you are really prolonging the "a" and not the "rrr." faaaaaar — not fauuuurr.

The function of the consonant is simply to *start* the vowels or to *stop* them. Sing for example, "toot," and notice the function of both t's. We may indeed call vowels the essence or soul of a word and the consonants the *vowel starters* or *vowel stoppers*.

Here are a few observations on vowels and consonants

a) Vowel sounds must be pure or homogenous. Make a test, sing the vowel "o" making sure this vowel does not close into "oo;" sing "a" (as in ate) making sure that the "a" does not become an "ee."

b) Note that single vowels are sometimes made up of two vowel *sounds*. Sing the word "right" sustaining the vowel a few seconds, and observe that the "i" consists of "ah" and "ee." Always remember that the *initial vowel sound* must be prolonged. And the other vowel sounds must come at the very end, right before the final consonant. Thus r-ah-ah-ah-ah-ah-eet. Not rah-ee-ee-ee-ee-t.

c) There are certain consonants that are capable of being sustained, and care must be taken that they are not. These consonants must be sounded sharp, crisp, and brief, like all consonants. Consonants like, b, k, d, t, etc., will give no problem in this respect because they are short by nature. But watch out for f, l, and especially r, and s. Their sustained prolongation does not yield a pleasant effect. Try for yourself to sing the words "hill," "stiff," "fur," and "hiss." By prolonging these final or terminal consonants, you will understand why their sound is objectionable. The problem of the "r" in "fur" is encountered more often in words ending "er," "mother," "ever." What exactly *is* the vowel sound in "er?" It is certainly not the usual guttural "r" sound heard too frequently in untutored voices. You must perceive that the vowel sound is a modified "eh" with the "r" a short, crisp, terminal sound at the end of the prolonged vowel.

(d) Three other sounds, capable of being prolonged, are not only unoffensive, but are actually beautiful in their musical effect. These are "m" and "n" and "ng." Sing the words "name," "moon," "and song," sustaining the final resonant consonants. Some popular singers like to hang on to these humming terminals, but in more orthodox renditions, these consonants are sounded only in brief duration.

MMMMMMM

In demonstrating here the importance of the sustained, unadulterated vowel together with the short, crispness of the consonants, there is no intention to slight the importance of the consonants. In fact, the very clarity of diction and the understandability of the words depends largely on the careful articulation of the consonants. The point to be remembered is that the vowel is that component of a syllable that is sustained or prolonged throughout the duration of the syllable save for the brief instant that the consonant initiates or stops the vowel sound. "Sing the vowel" is a good rule to remember. In fact when practicing singing exercises, students vocalize on vowels almost exclusively.

It might be well to insert here an admonition to sing those consonants capable of being voiced in pitch (m,n,l,r, and their combinations) on the same pitch as the vowels that combine with them in a syllable. For example, in the word "pray" the "pr" must not be sung lower or higher than the "ay;" the "pr" must be sounded on the same pitch level as the "ay."

A MODERN SINGING AID

In this affluent age when tape recorders are found in so many homes, it is certainly recommended that one avail oneself of the training value that this invaluable piece of equipment has to offer. No longer, like the singers of an older age, do we have to stand facing the corner of a room and extend our ears with cupped hands bending them forward slightly to test the reflected sound of our voice in order to hear ourselves as others do. Tape recorders are much too honest in their reproduction of our voice. The usual remark made by those hearing themselves for the first time on a tape recorder, "you sound like yourself, but I don't sound like myself," is convincing evidence that we do not hear ourselves as others hear us. However, the ruthless candor of the playback should serve to lead us to improvement rather than to discouragement.

Chapter 3

SIGHT-READING MELODIES

WHY JOHNNY CAN'T READ MUSIC

We are speaking of reading notes, of course. There is an illiteracy in music just as there is an illiteracy in words. And musical illiteracy is pitifully rife in America.

So don't feel too bad right now if "notes" are so many bothersome specks on a piece of paper, because you have plenty of company right in the same pew with you.

As a matter of fact, it is safe to assume that most singers in the average church choir use music notation more or less as a general guide in their singing. In other words, they "go up" when the notes go up, and "go down" when the notes go down, and stay the same when the notes do too. How *far* the notes go up or down is quite another matter. But the problem is usually taken care of by a good musical guess and the aid of a thumping piano. This method is sort of a combination of *rote* and *reading*. Indeed many skilled singers are quite satisfied with this method and usually feel it is not "worth the trouble" to learn to read notes more thoroughly — especially if there is no good teacher on hand to teach them. Their own talent and musical ear seem to compensate for their lack of training in this respect.

It is important to know that by "reading notes" we do *not* mean the ability to *name* the notes. We don't even mean the ability to *play* the notes on the piano, which is simply transferring the name of a note to the name of the corresponding key on the piano, according to a simple code system of matching the notes and the piano keys by letters of the alphabet. In other words, a certain note is called by the letter "a," in order to sound and strike the corresponding piano key that is also lettered "a." This is much like assembling a new piece of household furniture or a child's swing where the diagram instructions indicate where bolt "a" fits into slot "a" and so on. Now here is precisely the reason why Johnny can't read music. For nearly a decade of years, he is taught technical names of all kinds of musical notation from ancient Gregorian Chant to present-day notes. He knows what a staff is, the treble clef and porrectusflexus; he can name every note from "A" to "G" but he can't sing one of them.

As a matter of fact, those gifted (at birth) human beings, who are able to sound "A" or any other note without the aid of a musical instrument, are as rare as elephants at a Demo-

cratic convention. This chapter is not aimed at all the rest of us who "don't know one note from the other." Since notes by their letter names "A" or "B" do not register any corresponding pitch in our minds, and since these notes will be learned to sing rather than to play on a mechanical instrument, we shall not be concerned with the absolute sound of the notes.

We shall be concerned only with the *relative* sounds of the notes as expressed by the musical syllables, *do, re, mi, fa, sol, la, ti, do.* In other words all we want to learn is how much higher "A" is than "B," or "C" is than "F," and so on. We don't care what "A" sounds like in itself. There is an added advantage this way, for the singer, since he can choose his own pitch for "A," "B," or "C," to best suit his voice (which he probably insists is much lower than most songs are pitched).

Hence from now on we will dismiss the alphabet letters and concern ourselves only with *do, re, mi,* in naming the notes. Using this *do, re, mi* system is nothing new. It dates back to the eleventh century and it is still the most widely used system in America for those who sing at sight. Guido d'Arezzo, the monk who invented it, died in the year 1050. He devised it of course, only for singing. The particular type of singing was, of course, Gregorian Chant, the only church music in use at that time. In the Latin hymn, "Ut queant laxis," written in honor of St. John the Baptist in the tenth century, Guido observed that the initial note of each phrase was on a successive degree of the staff, the four lines on which music was written in his time.

The ingenious monk, knowing that the notes needed names anyway, saw here an opportunity to name them by simply giving them the syllables underlying them in the hymn. Some centuries after Guido's death, an Italian singer, Doni, found the syllable "ut" not as easy to sing as the rest of the syllables that ended in a vowel. So he changed the "ut" to "do," the initial syllable of his name. Guido's system is called "solmization" or "solfeggio." Since his time the square chant notation gradually developed into our modern notation after musical instruments were invented, and it became practical to have a

Ut que-ant lax-is

Re-so-na-re fi-bris

Mi- ra ges-to-rum

Fa mu-li tu-o-rum,

Sol-ve pol-lu-ti

La-bi-i-re-a-tum,

ut re mi fa sol la

fixed pitch for notes to satisfy the obvious need for uniformity. But in ancient times, musical notation was used for the human voice only. It behooves us now to simply interpret our modern musical notation in the same manner as the ancients did. This might seem like resisting progress — something like getting a horse to pull an automobile — but we simply cannot let these new-fangled musical instruments render obsolete the most ancient of all instruments, the human voice.

DO — A DEER

There is only one prerequisite for learning to sight-read music according to the plan in this chapter. You must be able to sing in tune the do scale: *do, re, mi, fa, sol, la, ti, do; do, ti, la, sol, fa, mi, re, do.*

Or, if you prefer:

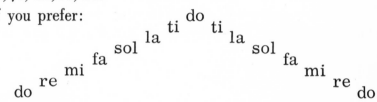

You must be able to sing this series of syllables both backward and forward (or up and down) by memory. If you cannot do that, close the book until you find someone to teach you; then come back and continue the book.
We'll wait.

I CAN DO IT,
I CAN DO IT!

Fine! Now that you can do it, let's proceed. First, see if you can discern that each tone in the scale *is not* equidistant in pitch from each other. You probably can't distinguish that slight difference in pitch just yet. So we will *tell* you that each step from one tone to another is the same in all cases except for two, namely: *mi* to *fa,* and *ti* to *do.* These are half the distance of the others. All the other steps progress in what we'll call "whole steps" or just "step" while *mi* progresses a "half step" to *fa,* and *ti* progresses a "half step" to *do.* Graphic illustrations below present a visual means of understanding the whole and half steps.

This existense of half steps and whole steps used in our musical system is simply a part of our western culture. And the *do* scale, starting and ending with *do,* sounds the way it does simply because of the position of the half steps or half-tones — namely: between steps 3 and 4 and 7 and 8.

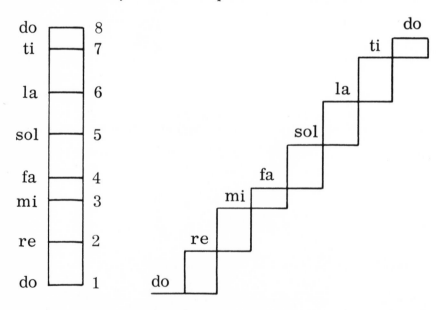

By a simple reduction of the scale ladder above to a smaller one in which we use the spaces as well as the lines to indicate musical steps, we have the familiar music staff.

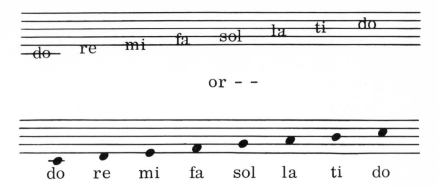

or - -

do　re　mi　fa　sol　la　ti　do

The degrees of the scale proceed from line to space and then to the next line, etc. Visually now the half tones are not distinguishable from the whole tones.

Now sight-singing is simply the ability to sing the notes of the scale mixed up. Mixed up in a particular order these notes of the scale can constitute a song or a melody. For example, sing the following: *mi, mi, mi, sol, sol, fa, mi;* and you are sight-singing the opening line of a familiar hymn which you will recognize as "Angels We Have Heard on High."

Actually you could sing all your melodies from the musical syllables spelled out this way, but it's much simpler when transferred to the staff and, as you will see later, the notes on the staff can also indicate rhythm besides pitch. (The stems on notes indicate rhythm, and since we are not concerned with rhythm at present, the notes used below are *without* their stems.)

ANGELS WE HAVE HEARD ON HIGH

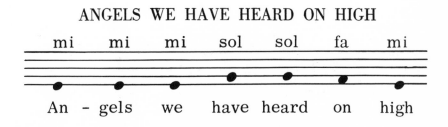

Notice how the above melody uses the lower part of the staff.

① Some melodies might run right off the staff and we would have to add more lines as we do in this famous Christmas carol: ② *to change pitch + key* ③

O COME ALL YE FAITHFUL

do	do	sol	do	re	sol

O   come   all   ye   faith - ful

The obvious way to circumvent this inconvenience is to simply place the syllable *do* higher up on the staff. In other words, when melodies extend pretty much below *do*, we place *do* higher up. When melodies extend above *do*, we place *do* on a lower degree. In other words, in certain pieces, *do* is moved to other degrees of the staff. That is why this is sometimes called the "moveable *do* system."

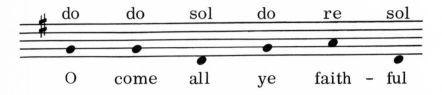

do   do   sol   do   re   sol

O   come   all   ye   faith - ful

In other words, *do* can be placed anywhere on the staff — which brings us to the question, "How do we know where *do* is when we see a piece of music?"

HOW TO FIND *DO* IN A SONG

A. This is a *sharp* ♯ . The degree of the staff that is affected by this sign is the line or space that is bounded by the two horizontal lines.

B. This is a *flat* ♭ . The degree of the staff that is affected by this sign is the line or space on which it is placed.

To find *do,* the following three rules need be remembered:

Rule 1: Where there are no sharps or flats — *do* is always on a ledger line added below the staff

do

and here,

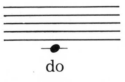

do

providing the treble clef 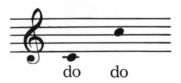 appears at the beginning of the line.

do   do

Rule 2: When there are one or more sharps (#) placed at the beginning of a piece, the sharp farthest to the right is always *ti*; hence *do* is the next degree up from the sharp.

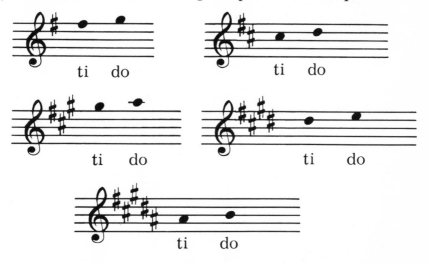

Rule 3: When there are flats (♭) placed at the beginning of a piece, the flat farthest to the right is always *fa*. Hence, *do* and any other note can be determind by counting the successive degrees from *fa*.

Now when you can find *do* in any composition, you can find the name of any note that appears on the staff simply by counting up or down from *do*. If, for example, you know that in a particular instance *do* is located on the first line of the staff,

do

and you wish to learn the name of the note on the fourth line of the staff, you simply recite up the scale from *do*: *do, re, mi, fa, sol, la, ti, do* — and find that the name of the note on the fourth line of the staff is, in this case, *sol*.

do   re   mi   fa   sol

This method works in the opposite direction too. If *do* is in the third space of the staff

do   and you wish

to know the syllable name of the note which is in the first space, simply recite down the scale from *do*: *do, ti, la, sol, fa* — and you will see that the syllable in the first space is *fa*.

do   ti   la   sol   fa

After you can *name* all the notes on this staff, you then should soon be able to sing them. And that, in short, is *sight-singing*.

Here is a practical way to go about sight-singing. First assume a comfortable pitch for *do*. If you see that the melody will rise rather high above *do*, take a note for *do* that is low in your particular range. If *do* is the highest point in the melody, take a note for *do* that is comfortably high for you. From this pitch of *do* that you have chosen, sing a few notes up or down the scale in tune until you have that *"do"* feeling. *Do* always has a feeling of finality or conclusion. Now to find the starting note of the piece, if it is a note other than *do*, simply sing up or down from *do* until you have the pitch of this starting note. For example, in the Christmas carol, "Silent Night," the starting note is *sol*. To sing this note, first assume a low pitch for *do*, then sing up the scale to *sol*. That is your starting note for "Silent Night."

Suppose we try to sing the following example now:

Assume a pitch for *do*. If you cannot spontaneously sing the next note *mi*, simply sing up the scale to *mi*: *do*, *re*, *mi*. Now sing *do*, *mi*, skipping the *re*. For a wider interval, follow the same procedure.

sol   mi

Assume a rather low pitch for *do*, and sing up to *sol*. Pause on *sol* in order to remember the pitch; then sing from *sol* up to *mi*, remembering the sound of *mi*. Now can you sing *sol*, *mi*, without sounding the intervening notes?

Try a descending example.

do   sol

DADDY SAYS HE'S TRYING TO REMEMBER "ME"

INTERVALS

Of course, we can't forever employ such a laborious way of finding the pitch of these skipped notes; we must learn to sing them outright. A few simple singing drills will help us. But from now on let us speak of the distance from one note to another as an *interval*. Singing from *do* to the same *do* in a simple repetition of the same sound is a "first' 'or better called a "prime," e.g.

PRIME

From any note to the note on the next degree of the staff (up or down) is a second. For example: *do, re; sol, la*; e.g.

SECONDS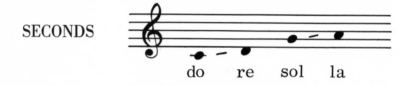

do   re   sol   la

From any note to the note two degrees away on the staff (skipping one degree on the staff) is a third. Thus: *do, mi*; *re, fa*. In other words, from one line to the next line or one space to the next space is a third.

THIRDS ASCENDING

do   mi   re   fa   mi   sol   fa   la

THIRDS DESCENDING

do   la   ti   sol   la   fa   sol   mi

Chords — Harmonic intervals
(all notes together)
Melodic Interval
(notes one after another)

Here are intervals of a fourth.   FOURTHS ASCENDING

do fa re sol mi la fa ti

FOURTHS DESCENDING

do sol ti fa la mi sol re

Other intervals can be determined in the same manner. Here are all the musical intervals:

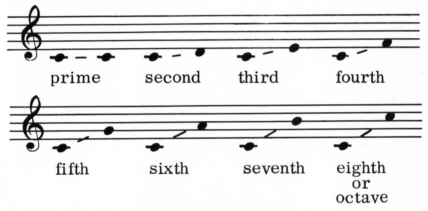

prime   second   third   fourth

fifth   sixth   seventh   eighth
or
octave

SHARPS AND FLATS

For our purpose, sharps or flats placed at the beginning of the piece simply perform the function of indicating where *do* is. But when a sharp or flat occurs in the course of a piece, it has the function of altering the pitch of the note before which it is placed: *DO + KEY*

A sharp raises a pitch a half tone.   A flat lowers a pitch a half tone.

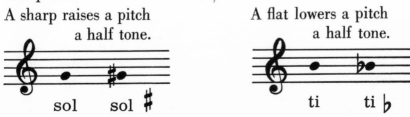

sol sol ♯   ti ti ♭

If you will recall, there are only two semi-tones in the scale, while all the rest are whole tones. Obviously it is possible to sing a pitch between the whole tones thus making a series of all semi-tones.

The marking (-·---------·) between notes indicates areas where pitches may be inserted between the whole tones.

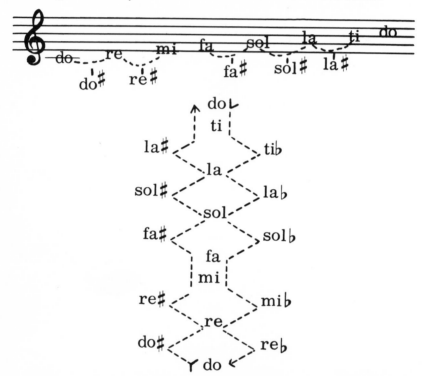

As is apparent in the above diagram, an altered note is sharped or flatted, depending on whether it is considered as the lower note raised or the upper note lowered. For example: *do* raised a half step, is *do sharp; re* lowered, is *re flat*. The two notes *do sharp* and *re flat* sound identical, even though they appear differently on the staff and have different names.

Placing tones between the whole tones creates half tones, the smallest musical interval recognized in our western musical system. It is impossible, of course, to insert a note between *mi* and *fa*, and *ti* and *do*, since these are already semi-tones.

For simplification in singing, the altered (raised or lowered) musical syllables are given one-syllable names by uniformly changing the vowels of the notes altered to the letter "i" in the case of raised syllables, and to "e" in the case of the flatted syllables.

The complete scale then with all its altered syllables, comprising all the tones used in musical composition, are illustrated in the following diagrams. Notes added above and below the scale of *do* to *do* are simply extensions of the scale upwards or downwards.

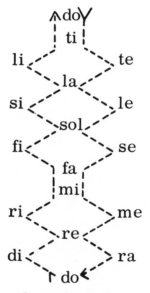

Since *re* already ends in "e," this syllable becomes *ra* when lowered.

On the music staff the above diagram looks like this:

la   li   ti   do   do   ti   te   la   le

sol   se   fa   mi   me   re   ra   do

If in a composition a note is to be restored to its normal or neutral state, a natural sign (♮) placed beside the note that was previously altered, will effect this change.

sol fi sol fa

In the following examples, *sol* is flatted in its normal state, since the flat occurs in the beginning of the line. Hence, it would require a double flat ($\flat\flat$) to lower *sol* to *se*, and a natural sign to raise it to *si*.

sol se si

Observe how the accidentals affect the various notes in the following examples:

mi sol me di do

la de ti di

In hymns and psalms that the people sing, the most frequently encountered accidental is *fi*. It might be well to practice this peculiar progression.

sol fi sol fa

BY GOLLY
I THINK HE'S
GOT IT!

Chapter 4

RHYTHM

BEATS AND TIME MEASUREMENT

When you sing a familiar song, you will notice that some words or syllables are held longer than others. Some are short and some are long. In order to ascertain precisely how much longer some notes are prolonged in relation to other notes, we must measure them. In order to do this, we do not take out our watch and time each note, we simply tap our foot or our finger. Our movements in "keeping time" are steady, evenly spaced "beats" that actually perform a function similar to that of a clock. Indeed, if we were singing a song, the beat of which would occur sixty times to a minute, we would actually be measuring our notes in seconds without being aware of it.

The relative duration of one note to another is the principle we call *rhythm*. In other words, rhythm concerns itself with how *long* we hold one note in relation to another note. And, as said before, we measure this length of time, this duration, by a regular beat.

In some songs the beat is fast as in a gay dance tune; sometimes the beat is slow as in a funeral dirge. This *speed* of the beat, which in music we call *tempo*, is not to be confused with *rhythm*. Remember, rhythm concerns itself with *how long* one note is held in relation to another, whether these notes be measured by a regular *fast* beat or a regular *slow* beat.

Another element of music not to be confused with rhythm, though it is intimately connected with it, is "accent." We refer to some songs as having a "strong beat," and in fact in almost all songs one beat will be found to be stronger or heavier than the others. This accented beat you can feel very well in a waltz like "East Side, West Side" or a march like "I've Been Working On the Railroad." What might otherwise be a monotonous series of uniform beats becomes a waltz when every third beat is accented, and becomes a march when every fourth beat is accented. Regardless of these regularly recurring accents on every third, fourth and second beat, these same beats still perform their primary function in measuring the length of each note.

Rhythm ⟶

Metrical :
) *fixed unit of time* 4/4, *etc*.
) *orderly arrangement (regular accents) recurring*

Free :
1) *no fixed time*
2) *no reg. accent*

regular + irregular accents (Syncopation)

GLO ⟶

It is one thing to tap our feet or sway our bodies — in short, to "feel the beat" of a military band or of a dance band. In this instance the music is performed by others, and the beat that is an inherent element of the music and at the same time keeps the band together, is transmitted to us. It is quite another thing to adopt a beat and perform a piece of music in the proper rhythm — especially if we are unfamiliar with the music. In order to do this we must be able to read notes and interpret or perform the rhythm of these notes.

Up to this time we interpreted only the pitch of the notes which was indicated on the various degrees of the five-lined staff by the oval portion of the notes. Now we must interpret the rhythm of the notes by the following:

1) The stem:

2) Black or white notes:

3) The dot:

Here in the order of decreasing length are all the types of notes that convey various rhythms:

This series could be extended by adding more "flags" to notes such as , ; but the five notes above are practically all we ever use in vocal music. The meaning of the dot will be considered in later paragraphs.

At this time, let us consider <u>the relative length</u> or duration of the above notes even before we speak of their names by which we identify them.

1) a fixed relationship

In the diagram below each note is double the value (in time) of the note to its immediate right.

always constant proportion

𝅝 , 𝅗𝅥 , 𝅘𝅥 , 𝅘𝅥𝅮 , 𝅘𝅥𝅯 , 𝅘𝅥𝅲

Therefore, each note, reading from right to left, is half the value of the note to its left.

Experiment: Sing the syllable "ta" to the two notes below, sustaining the first note twice as long as the second note.

𝅗𝅥   𝅘𝅥

ta ——— ta ——

2) variable value :
metronome
time signature

The only practical way to measure the two notes above is by a beat: two beats for 𝅗𝅥 , one beat for 𝅘𝅥 . (Arrows indi-

↑↑   ↑

cate beats.) Mathematically speaking, it doesn't matter how many beats one note is given as long as the other is given half as many. Hence in the above instance we can measure the two notes by giving four beats for the first note and two beats for the second.

(fast
quarter
note
or
slow one)
(eighth
gets one
beat

𝅗𝅥   𝅘𝅥

ta ———————— ta ——

↑   ↑   ↑   ↑   ↑   ↑

Sing only one "ta" to each note, not to each beat. The "ta" should be sung but once throughout the duration of each note regardless of how many beats (indicated by the arrow) the note receives.

or
half
receives
one beat
etc.)

SOUNDS
LIKE
MATH!

Important note: The duration of one beat lasts until the next begins. Considering that the foot or hand tap is short in itself, the space between each tap must be part of the previous beat. In other words the tap is simply the beginning of the beat and the beat lasts until the next tap begins. This principle is sometimes overlooked even by professional musicians. For example, to give a note *one* beat we really need *two* taps — the first to start the beat, and the second to end it. Example: to give the note ♩ one beat we must begin "ta" on the first beat and sustain "ta" until the second beat begins.

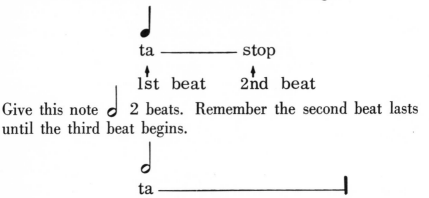

Give this note ♩ 2 beats. Remember the second beat lasts until the third beat begins.

Let's name the notes so we can refer to them properly. Since each note is held twice as long as the note on its right, we need simply call the first note a "whole note" and the rest of the names follow logically: half note, quarter note, eighth note, sixteenth note.

Let us now observe some relationships between the notes according to extremely rudimentary principles of arithmetic.

Here is another self-explanatory picture:

From the tables above, it follows that

If 𝅘𝅥𝅮 receives one beat, { 𝅗𝅥 receives 2 beats.

𝅝 receives 4 beats.

If 𝅘𝅥 receives one beat, { 𝅗𝅥 receives 2 beats.

𝅝 receives 4 beats.

If 𝅗𝅥 receives one beat, 𝅝 receives 2 beats.

Notice that if we lift the stems to be a series of eighth notes 𝅘𝅥𝅮 𝅘𝅥𝅮 𝅘𝅥𝅮 𝅘𝅥𝅮 and join them together ♫♫ we can depict these notes in a clearer manner.

↑
7 of them

Giving one beat to the quarter note, sing "ta" to the following exercise:

♩ ♩ ♩ ♩

ta ta ta ta

↑ ↑ ↑ ↑

Simple ones :
I
II
III

Remember to give two beats to the half note, four beats to the whole note.
Try this one.

♩ ♩ ♩ ♩ ♩ o

ta ta ta   ta ta ta

↑ ↑ ↑↑ ↑ ↑ ↑ ↑ ↑ ↑

Let us look again at all the various notes:

o ♩ ♩ ♪ ♪

and consider the relationship between the longest and the shortest of these:

o = ♪ ♪ ♪ ♪ ♪ ♪ ♪ ♪ ♪ ♪ ♪ ♪ ♪ ♪ ♪ ♪

If we beat one to ♪, we should have to beat sixteen to a o , an impractical situation. If we beat one to ♩ , we would beat only four to a o and the ♪ would receive a quarter of a beat. The problem is: how can we sing for only a quarter of a beat, or even a half a beat? If ♩ receives one beat, ♪ receives a half beat; or, ♩   ♪ Drill:

↑   ↑

Sing "ta," giving one beat to ♩

♩ ♩ ♩ ♩ ♪ ♪ ♪ ♪ ♩ ♩ ♩

ta ta ta ta ta ta ta ta ta ta ta end

↑ ↑ ↑ ↑ ↑ ↑ ↑ ↑ ↑ ↑↑↑↑

Try this one. The vertical lines (bar lines) divide notes into four beats.

ta   ta ta   ta   ta ta

1   2   3   4

         end

ta ta ta ta   ta ta ta   ta———

1   2   3   4   1 2 3 4 1

Try four "ta's" to one beat.

ta   ta ta ta ta   ta   ta   ta——ta   ta ta ta ta

1   2   3   4 1 2 3   4

ta   ta ta   ta   ta   ta_____

1   2   3   4   1   2   3   4

MY RESPECT
FOR MUSICIANS
IS GROWING
RAPIDLY

TIME SIGNATURES

At the beginning of many pieces of music there usually appear two numerals placed above each other in the manner of a fraction.

The top numeral indicates how *many* notes, the bottom numeral what *kind* of note, in a measure. In other words, $\frac{2}{4}$ means that there are two quarter notes to a measure. $\frac{3}{4}$ means three quarter notes to a measure, and so on.

Usually the bottom numeral also indicates what kind of note receives one beat. $\frac{3}{4}$ would mean that there are three quarter notes to a measure and the quarter note receives one beat.

THE TIE AND THE DOTTED NOTES

A tie ⌒ joining 2 notes together on the same degree of the staff increases the duration or time value of the first tied note by the value of the second note, without the second note being sounded.

The dot (.) appearing beside a note ♩., ♩. increases the duration of that note by half its original value.

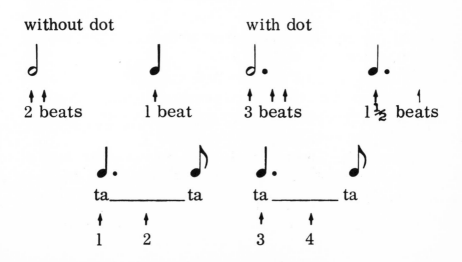

An excellent way to understand the execution of the dotted note is by relating it to the tied note.

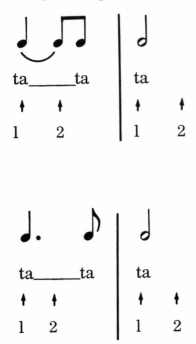

ta_____ta ta

↑   ↑ ↑   ↑

1   2 1   2

The dot takes the place of the tied eighth note in this illustration, and receives (the first half of) the second beat.

ta_____ta ta

↑   ↑ ↑   ↑

1   2 1   2

Sing "ta" while tapping out the beats to the following:

ta ta ta ta

↑ ↑ ↑ ↑

ta ta ta ta ta ta ta ta ta

↑ ↑   ↑ ↑   ↑ ↑   ↑ ↑   ↑↑↑↑

The Tie and the Dotted Eighth Note

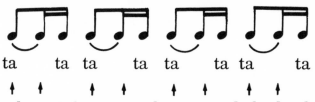

ta   ta ta   ta ta   ta ta   ta

Perhaps it is better to beat twice as many beats to the eighth notes in order to more accurately execute the fast sixteenth notes. In other words we subdivide the beat.

ta   ta ta   ta ta   ta ta   ta

The above tied notes can be expressed also by the dotted eighth note. The dot might be considered to be taking the place of the tied sixteenth notes.

ta   ta   ta   ta   ta   ta   ta   ta

59

In the following exercises be sure to distinguish between the double eighth notes 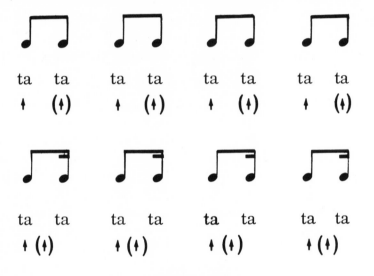 and the dotted eighth note with its sixteenth note.

The subdivided beat or half beat is indicated in parentheses. This half beat is also expressed in the lifting of the hand or the raising of the foot, when tapping out the beats.

ta ta   ta ta   ta ta   ta ta

↑ (↑)   ↑ (↑)   ↑ (↑)   ↑ (↑)

ta ta   ta ta   ta ta   ta ta

↑ (↑)   ↑ (↑)   ↑ (↑)   ↑ (↑)

RESTS

There are silences in music just as there are sounds; and these silences are measured in the same way as the sounds are. <u>Measured silences</u> in music are called rests. There is a rest equivalent in time value to each kind of note, and the names of the rests are the same as their corresponding notes.

whole rest	𝄻	𝅝	whole note
half rest	𝄼	𝅗𝅥	half note
quarter rest	𝄽	𝅘𝅥	quarter note
eighth rest	𝄾	𝅘𝅥𝅮	eighth note
sixteenth rest	𝄿	𝅘𝅥𝅯	sixteenth note

A whole rest receives as many beats as does a whole note, a half rest receives as many beats as a half note, and so on.

Sing "ta" to the notes, and be silent during the rests in the following exercise. Continue beating however, through the notes and rests alike.

End of 3rd quarter

Chapter 5

THE SONGS WE SING

OUR BACKGROUND

Before 1964, when the Mass was still in Latin, most of our hymn-singing was done outside of Mass, during holy hours, novenas, and the like. The hymns even for those services, were not of the highest merit, as any scrutiny of the words and the melody will show. These two elements, words and melody, are the two principal components of any song, and both of them must be considered in our judgment.

So much condemnation has been made in the past of the old Catholic hymn favorites, that it would be redundant to add more here. Rather let us consider the more meritorious hymns of the past and the new songs of the immediate future. And let us endeavor to form standards by which we ourselves can make adequate judgments concerning the sacred music we sing in church. We use "songs" in a generic way, for "hymns" as well as "psalms" are two of the several *types* of "songs" used in divine worship.

HYMNS

A hymn might be defined as a simple song whose words are metered and rhymed according to one of the conventional verse patterns. In other words, each line of a hymn has a definite word-accent pattern that can be expressed rhythmically in the manner of taDUM, taDUM, taDUM, For example; let us look at two verses of the hymn, "To Jesus Christ, Our Sovereign King."

To Je- sus Christ, our sov- 'reign King,   a
ta DUM ta DUM ta DUM ta DUM

Who is the world's Sal - va - tion,   b
ta DUM ta DUM ta DUM ta

All praise and hom- age do we bring   a
ta DUM ta DUM ta DUM ta DUM

And thanks and ad- o- ra- tion.   b
ta DUM ta DUM ta DUM ta

Thy reign ex- tend, O King be- nign,   c
ta DUM ta DUM ta DUM ta DUM

To ev- 'ry land and na- tion;   b
ta DUM ta DUM ta DUM ta

For in thy king dom, Lord di- vine,   c
ta DUM ta DUM ta DUM ta DUM

A- lone we find sal- va- tion.   b
ta DUM ta DUM ta DUM ta

The number of syllables in each line, with definite recurring accented and unaccented syllables, shows the particular meter or measure of the hymn. The rhyme scheme is a,b,a,b, c,b,c,b. It is "stanzaic" in that each stanza is of identical rhythm and can thus be sung to the same melody to which the first stanza is sung.

Here we can see that the hymn, as a type of religious song, has obvious advantages in its simplicity. The rhythm and rhyme schemes are effective aids for learning and memorizing the words. No matter how many stanzas there are to the hymn, the melody in the first stanza is all one needs to learn; the same short tune of the first stanza serves for the entire length of the song.

WHAT RHYMES WITH HOLY?

Regrettably these same savory ingredients of meter and rhyme impose severe limitations upon the freedom and imagination of hymn-lyric writers. There are just so many words in the English language that rhyme, and most of these have been paired so often that they are already beyond the point of triteness. Serious poets have long ago abandoned the conventional verse and rhythmic patterns in order that they may have more freedom in their expression. But our hymn writers cannot shake off these binding restrictions, because a hymn, in order to be a hymn, must be metered and rhymed. All the more skill is demanded of our poets, if, within these strict forms, they must yet achieve originality, literary art, and theological truth. *What is said* in a hymn, and *how it is said* are the two most important elements by which a hymn text must be judged. Pietistic nonsense and surface sentimentality must not usurp the place of sacred truths and profound religious feeling. Modern day Christians must become mature in their discrimination between good and bad texts in religious songs. Scripture and tradition, which form our modern day theology, are always the most reliable basis for the thought content of our hymns.

SOURCE OF OUR PRESENT HYMNS

It must be remembered that the Latin rite of the Roman Church could hardly foster any great treasury of English hymns. But the Protestant Church did. Since the time of the Reformation there have been composed tunes and texts that have now reached an accumulation of quite a sizeable anthology. Many hundreds of Protestant hymns are now extant. Some of these texts are translations of older Latin hymns, and many of the melodies are taken literally from the most ancient sources.

The incipient stages of the Catholic liturgical reform seem to coincide in time with the beginning of the Ecumenical Movement. Perhaps, if the one did not start the other, they at least mutually fostered each other. At any rate, a felicitous coincidence it was, and the part music played in the growth of these movements cannot be overestimated.

The need for hymns in the liturgical reform was an immediate one. Then what could have been more simple than to draw from the hymnbooks of our Protestant brethren! In the first place, a great portion of the Protestant hymns were more Catholic in doctrine than were the Catholic hymns in current use at the time. Even had there not been a great need for

English hymns in the new liturgy, many of the Protestant classics, because of their great intrinsic merit, should have been admitted to our Catholic hymnals long ago.

An historic event in hymnody and ecumenism was the appearance in 1954 of the *PEOPLE'S HYMNAL*. A rather thin and inexpensive booklet, it was the first Catholic hymnal to include the more standard Protestant hymns, both words and music. It was also the first Catholic hymnal to include a sizeable portion of grand newly composed Catholic hymns, and the first *not* to include any of the less meritorious Catholic favorites.

At that time it was difficult enough to gain ecclesiastical approval for the prudent selection of Protestant hymns in that first edition of the *PEOPLE'S HYMNAL*; it would have been a scandalous disaster to include the more glaring hymns that smacked of Protestantism. Only ten years later, after ecumenism began to flourish, could a hymn attributed to Luther himself — especially his "A Mighty Fortress" — be boldly admitted to the *PEOPLE'S MASS BOOK*. In the decades following the first edition of the *PEOPLE'S HYMNAL*, nearly all other Catholic hymnals have included these same Protestant hymns, and most Catholics are hardly aware of their Protestant origin.

A few words might be inserted here concerning the hymn "A Mighty Fortress," since this hymn has raised more Catholic eyebrows than any other Protestant hymn. Because "A Mighty Fortress" was practically the theme song of the Protestant Reformation, one would naturally assume that strong anti-Catholic sentiments would be expressed in the words. This is not the case. Then "why," one might ask, is there a new text for the Catholic version now being sung in our churches? Simply because the present Protestant version is written in antiquated language, e.g., "For still our ancient folk, doth seek to work us woe." Furthermore, one must remember that the original text of "A Mighty Fortress" was written in German. The present Protestant English versions are vague translations of the original. The text, attributed to Martin Luther, is presumably based on "Psalm 45." The new Catholic version then, is simply a version more accurately following a modern translation of "Psalm 45." Along with the opening two lines, the hymn retains a few of the other characteristic lines of the popular Protestant version.

It is a plain fact that nearly all the popular Protestant hymns, the words especially, were written in the nineteenth century; and their Victorian flavor is becoming more and more unsavory to the taste of our present decade in the twentieth century. Updating existing texts is oftentimes impossible without rewriting the entire lyric. In the case of the great hymn texts that have attained a classical stature, it would seem that they should be left unaltered in spite of their obsolescent language. Shakespeare is archaic; but it would be an unpardonable crime to alter him.

What seems to be an axiom in Protestant hymnody is that new hymn lyrics are being written continuously, but only to be sung to the old tunes. Congregations do not mind the new words, but they are averse to learning new tunes. This is understandable since the words can be read at sight, but the new melodies, hardly ever! Catholic congregations, centuries behind in a singing tradition, have a vast repertory of standard hymns to catch up with. In addition to learning many fine Protestant tunes, they will undoubtedly be confronted by a continuous stream of new lyrics and music flowing from the pens of our creative artists.

WHAT
DO YOU
MEAN
NEW HYMNS?
THAT WAS
WRITTEN IN
THE 15TH
CENTURY

If the music of our present hymns, drawn anywhere from the fifteenth to the twentieth centuries, seems unappealing to our twentieth century musical tastes, it may be attributed to the fact that these tunes are still new and unfamiliar. Our present era is one of transition and experiment. Perhaps out of our contemporary creativity there will someday evolve a musical idiom that is fully expressive of our modern American people in the sung worship of their Creator.

PSALMS

The psalms, those ancient prayers of the Old Testament, constitute most of the official prayer of the Roman liturgy. The English translations of these scriptural texts are almost always in prose; hence the text and the music to which they are set, are not metrical as in the case of a hymn.

The chief difficulty for composers lies in inventing a flexible musical *formula* to which all the verses — each of varying line length and number of syllables — can be sung. If a psalm melody were continuous, and thereby different for each verse, it would be impractical because of the difficulty in learning the long melody.

The words of the psalms might be completely strange and often unmeaningful to modern Americans on first reading. For centuries Catholics have heard these psalms in Latin, since they form the main prayer structure of the Mass. If they were unmeaningful in Latin, one might wonder if they are any more meaningful in English. However, one has but to realize that these psalms were the prayer of the ancient Hebrews, the chosen people of God, before the time of Christ, and a whole horizon of salvation history opens before one's eyes. A deep awareness of the roots of our Catholic faith shall come upon all who sing these prayers. The same psalms that were on the lips of King David were also on the lips of Our Lord, and now are upon our very own lips. Ancient though they are, the psalms are as fresh and pertinent in our times as they were when they were composed. We do not know to what melody the psalms were originally sung, but the words, in English translation, are the same.

As the present day people of God, God's chosen ones, we share the prayers of the Hebrews of old, whose religion was the foundation and the prelude to our own; for we inherit the Promise made to them by the same God of Abraham and Jacob.

Obscure passages and unfamiliar names should foster in us an intellectual curiosity that will lead to further study of our faith. Deep and rich will be the reward. And in turn we shall more and more grow in our appreciation of the psalms.

Of course there are predictable quips that will ensue when ancient imagery confronts the modern American mind. Take the married choir singers, for example, who sang for the first time these words from "Psalm 126," "your children shall be olive plants." The young father remarked he was going home to spank his "olive plants." And the young mother could not come to choir practice the next week unless she could find an "olive plant sitter."

May the psalms enrich our prayer life, increase our understanding of ancient Jewish history, and provide a few good laughs at the same time.

WHY WE DON'T SING

The noted critic, Paul Hume, in a recent address, pointed out that the American male on the way to one of his fraternal social gatherings might gaily join in a chorus of "Get Me To The Church On Time;" but after he once gets there, he is stone silent.

Belgian-born, Father Boniface Luykx, the great liturgist and African missionary, makes frequent trips to the United States. His observation is that the American people are exceptionally friendly and community-minded in their social living, *until* they cross the threshold of the church. Then they become individuals, silent, and alone, completely unmindful of their brethren beside them with whom they have been called together by God to worship as his family.

Silence in the church has no doubt been over-cultivated among American Catholics. They are horribly frightened at the prospect of hearing their own voice even in song.

Is America really a singing nation? How does it compare with other lands? In church, home, school, city functions, public defense, how do we Americans compare with people from other lands? Two instances, actual happenings during World War II, might serve to provide some answers to these questions.

The first was in Germany at the Elbe River during the closing days of the war, when American soldiers reached the eastern banks of the river and were awaiting the advancing Russian armies coming from the opposite direction toward the western bank. Weary, hard-pressed German troops, beaten and footsore, fled before their Russian pursuers. They had a preference as to what nation they would surrender to. They wanted the Americans as captors rather than the Russians.

For days the endless stream of German troops crossed over hastily-repaired broken bridges, dipping into the river, in order to give themselves up in the American-occupied town. Through the cobblestone streets, the Wermacht Army marched — hungry, dirty, disheveled, and defeated; but their heads were not hung low. They were held erect singing lustily the marching songs that thrilled the spirits of both the American soldiers and the German populace. Their weary retreat looked more like a parade. A hasty gulp of water handed to them by sympathetic women lining the streets was the only interruption to their song. The songs that all Germans knew by heart rose in manly harmony to break the tension of these dramatic and historic moments. In bitter defeat these German soldiers sang more heartily than Americans would sing in victory.

In their training days American G.I.'s were encouraged to brighten their long hikes by singing. But they seldom did. It seemed somehow that the command to sing was one military order difficult to obey and hard to enforce. Many an American colonel would like to have had his regiment known as "the singing regiment."

LET'S SING A SONG

Another instance. The scene was in Holland at a church-sponsored dance for American G.I.'s who were enjoying a three-day rest period as a respite from front-line foxhole duty. Comely Dutch maidens made ideal dancing partners, and their parents and townsfolk were genial hosts as well as chaperones. Like any proper church and civic event, the dance closed around midnight when the orchestra gave that subtle hint by intoning the national anthems. First it was the Dutch National Anthem. Just recently liberated, the jubilant and grateful Dutch sang their song with a fervor that vibrated not only the rafters but one's heart strings as well. The next song everybody knew would be the "Star Spangled Banner." The only Americans present of course, were the G.I.'s. One could not help but be apprehensive as to how the G.I.'s could handle their national anthem in comparison to the resounding Dutch performance. The American song followed, and what a surprise! The singing was every bit as full-throated as the first song. In fact, if there was a decibel of difference in the volume or the quality of the two songs, it was in favor of "O Say Can You See." Every Dutch citizen in the hall was singing at the top of his voice— the "Star Spangled Banner." The Dutch knew every word and every note by heart, and above all, they knew how to sing from the heart.

Occasions for national anthem singing in America do not compare too favorably with the above incident. At a civic or sporting event, be it a political convention, a baseball game, or a boxing match, who sings the S.S.B.? The assembled throng of spectators? No, a hired professional soloist singing over a microphone. And the sound of some of these professional songsters is sometimes not too inspiring. Their singing skill, it would seem, could be surpassed by some truck driver sitting out in the audience.

Many causes for an unsinging America can be readily offered. Standard and valid excuses are that television, radio, movies, phonograph records and juke boxes leave singing to a handful of professional entertainers who make passive listeners out of all the rest of us. The sensitivity of our listening ears is dulled by the relentless, never-ending music that crowds the air waves in homes, super-markets, buses and picnic grounds. Find a secluded forest, desert, or mountain-top; and if there is not a loud speaker speaking loud music, you will find a desperate teenager clutching a transistor radio. Music has become a drug that we need more and more in greater quantities —cruder, louder and noisier all the time. We Americans are the most song-loving people on earth so long as someone else is doing the singing! Our dulled listening ears are as overdeveloped as a weight lifter's biceps, while our singing voices are becoming as atrophied as the two front feet on a fish.

So if the American people do not sing at the fireside or in the automobile, they are not going to suddenly burst forth in hymns of praise at Sunday Mass.

Could it be then that instead of carrying song from our homes, schools, or taverns into the church, the reverse will happen in America? Perhaps our singing will begin in church, where the songs will rise like that thunderous sea, and some-day overflow even into our homes, our automobiles, and our picnics, until the time comes when that wobbly soprano who sings the S.S.B. over a microphone is finally put out of a job.